MACMILLAN
**ELEMEN**

OSCAR WILDE

# The Canterville Ghost
# and Other Stories

Retold by Stephen Colbourn

**MACMILLAN**
CLASSICS

**ELEMENTARY LEVEL**

*Founding Editor:* John Milne

Macmillan Guided Readers provide a choice of enjoyable reading material for all learners of English. The series comprises three categories: MODERNS, CLASSICS and ORIGINALS. Macmillan **Classics** are retold versions of internationally recognised literature, published at four levels of grading – Beginner, Elementary, Intermediate and Upper. At **Elementary Level**, the control of content and language has the following main features:

### Information Control

Stories have straightforward plots and a restricted number of main characters. Information which is vital to the understanding of the story is clearly presented and repeated when necessary. Difficult allusion and metaphor are avoided and cultural backgrounds are made explicit.

### Structure Control

Students will meet those grammatical features which they have already been taught in their elementary course of studies. Other grammatical features occasionally occur with which the students may not be so familiar, but their use is made clear through context and reinforcement. This ensures that the reading as well as being enjoyable provides a continual learning situation for the students. Sentences are kept short – a maximum of two clauses in nearly all cases – and within sentences there is a balance of simple adverbial and adjectival phrases. Great care is taken with pronoun reference.

### Vocabulary Control

At **Elementary Level** there is a limited use of carefully controlled vocabulary of approximately 1100 basic words. At the same time, students are given some opportunity to meet new or unfamiliar words in contexts where their meaning is obvious. The meaning of words introduced in this way is reinforced by repetition. Help is also given to the students in the form of vivid illustrations which are closely related to the text.

# Contents

# A Note About the Author

Oscar Wilde was born in Dublin, Ireland in 1854. He died in Paris in 1900. Many of the stories, plays and poems that Oscar Wilde wrote are still popular.

Stories: *The Picture of Dorian Gray, Lord Arthur Savile's Crime and Other Stories, The Happy Prince and Other Tales.*

Plays: *Lady Windermere's Fan, A Woman of No Importance, An Ideal Husband, The Importance of Being Earnest.*

Poems and Essays: *The Ballad of Reading Gaol, Ravenna, De Profundis.*

# THE
# CANTERVILLE
# GHOST

# THE CANTERVILLE GHOST

Mr Hiram B. Otis was a rich American from New York. He had come to live and work in England, but he did not want to live in London. He did not want to live in the city. He wanted to live in the countryside outside London.

Canterville Chase was a large and very old house near London. Lord Canterville, the owner, wanted to sell it. So Mr Hiram B. Otis visited Lord Canterville.

'I do not live in Canterville Chase,' Lord Canterville said to Mr Otis. 'I do not want to live there. The house has a ghost – The Canterville Ghost.'

'I come from America,' said Mr Otis. 'America is a modern country. I don't believe in ghosts. Have you seen this Canterville Ghost?'

'No,' said Lord Canterville, 'but I have heard it at night.'

'I don't believe in ghosts,' Mr Otis said again. 'No one has found a ghost. No one has put a ghost in a museum. And you haven't seen this ghost either.'

'But several members of my family have seen it,' said Lord Canterville. 'My aunt saw the ghost. She was so frightened that she was ill for the rest of her life. Also, the servants have seen it so they will not stay in the house at night. Only the housekeeper, Mrs Umney, lives in Canterville Chase. Mrs Umney lives there alone.'

'I want to buy the house,' said Mr Otis. 'I'll buy the ghost as well. Will you sell Canterville Chase? Will you sell the ghost?'

'Yes, I will,' said Lord Canterville. 'But, please remember, I told you about the ghost before you bought the house.'

———

Mr Hiram B. Otis bought Canterville Chase. Then his family came to England from America. He had a wife called Lucretia, three sons and a daughter.

The eldest son, Washington, was almost twenty years old. He was good-looking and had fair hair. His two young brothers were twins. They were twelve years old. The daughter, Virginia, was fifteen years old. She had large blue eyes and a lovely face.

Mr Otis took his family to live at Canterville Chase. The old house was in the countryside west of London. Mr Otis and his family travelled from London by train. Then they rode to the house in a wagon pulled by two horses.

Canterville Chase was big and old. Trees grew all around the house. The Otis family wanted to stop and look at the outside of the house, but the sky darkened. A thunderstorm was coming. Rain started to fall, so the family went inside the house quickly.

Mrs Umney, the housekeeper, was waiting for them by the front door. She was an old woman and wore a black dress and white apron. She lived at Canterville Chase and looked after the house.

'Welcome to Canterville Chase,' said Mrs Umney. 'Would you like some tea?'

'Yes, please,' said Mrs Otis.

The Otis family followed Mrs Umney into the library. There was a big table in the centre of the room and many chairs. Mrs Umney put teacups on the table, then she brought a pot of tea.

The Otises sat in the library and drank their tea. They looked out of a large window at the rain. The rain was falling heavily and the sky was black. They heard thunder and they saw lightning.

Mrs Otis looked around the room. There were many books on bookshelves. There were paintings on the walls. There was also a red stain on the floor. The red stain was by the fireplace.

'What is this red stain?' Mrs Otis asked Mrs Umney.

'It is blood,' answered the old housekeeper in a quiet voice.

'I don't want a blood-stain in my library,' said Mrs Otis. 'Please remove the stain. Please clean the floor immediately.'

The old woman smiled. 'It is the blood of Lady Eleanore de Canterville. She was murdered by her husband, Sir Simon de Canterville, in 1575. The blood-stain has been here for over three hundred years. It cannot be removed.'

'Nonsense,' said Washington Otis. 'I have some Pinkerton's Stain Remover from America. It can remove any stain. Watch.'

Washington Otis took the stain remover from a bag. Pinkerton's Stain Remover looked like a small black stick. He rubbed the stick on the blood-stain. A minute later the floor was clean. The stick had removed the stain quickly and easily.

Mrs Umney looked at the floor. She was frightened. No one had removed the blood-stain for three hundred years. Mrs Umney was very frightened.

'Pinkerton's can remove anything,' said Washington Otis. 'The blood-stain has gone.'

Lightning flashed and lit the library. Thunder crashed over the house. Mrs Umney fainted.

Mr and Mrs Otis ran across the library. They helped the old housekeeper who lay on the floor. Mrs Umney's eyes were closed and her face was pale.

'Mrs Umney! Mrs Umney!' cried Mrs Otis. 'Can you speak?'

Mrs Umney opened her eyes. 'Trouble will come to this house,' she said. 'I have seen the ghost. The ghost will come to you.'

All the Otises helped Mrs Umney to stand up. 'The ghost will come,' she said again. 'You must not remove the blood-stain. You must not clean the library floor. The ghost will be angry.'

Then Mrs Umney went upstairs to her room.

*Washington Otis rubbed Pinkerton's Stain Remover
on the blood-stain.*

'Let's look for the ghost,' said the Otis boys. 'Let's look round the house.'

The Otises looked round the house together. But they did not see the Canterville Ghost.

———

That night the family went to bed early. The storm continued all night. Next morning they went into the library. The blood-stain had reappeared on the floor.

'I'll remove this blood-stain once more,' said Washington Otis. 'Mother doesn't want a blood-stain in the library. I'll clean the floor again.'

He removed the blood-stain with Pinkerton's Stain Remover. The library floor was clean. But the next morning the stain had come back again.

'This is very strange,' said Mr Otis. 'I'll lock the library door at night. No one can come into the library. No one can put a stain on the floor.'

'I don't think Pinkerton's Stain Remover is bad,' said Washington Otis. 'I think there really is a ghost. The ghost is making the blood-stain. The ghost puts the stain on the floor at night.'

'We must find this ghost,' said Mr Hiram B. Otis. 'It must stop making these stains. Your mother does not like blood on the library floor.'

That day the family went out. They walked around the countryside near Canterville Chase. They went to the nearby village. They looked at the old village houses. Then they walked back to Canterville Chase through the woods. It was a summer evening and the weather was fine.

It was late when they got back to the house. The Otises were hungry and tired. After eating supper they went to bed. The bedrooms were upstairs. There was a long corridor upstairs. The bedroom doors were along this corridor.

Mr Otis woke up after midnight. There was a strange noise outside his room. The sound was like metal chains. The chains were rubbing together.

Mr Otis got out of bed and opened the bedroom door. He looked into the corridor.

He saw the Canterville Ghost in the corridor. The ghost was an old man with burning red eyes. He had long grey hair and wore very old-fashioned clothes. There were chains on his hands and feet. He was rubbing the chains together so they made a noise.

'My dear sir, your chains make a terrible noise,' Mr Otis said to the ghost. 'You must put some oil on those chains. Here is some Tammany Rising Sun Oil from the United States. Please put the oil on your chains.'

Mr Otis put a bottle of oil on a table in the corridor. Then he closed his bedroom door and went back to bed.

The Canterville Ghost was very surprised. He had lived in Canterville Chase for three hundred years. Everyone was frightened of him, because everyone was afraid of ghosts. But this American gentleman was not afraid.

The Canterville Ghost decided to work harder. He wanted to frighten the American. He made a terrible noise and shone a horrible green light in the corridor.

Another door opened at the end of the corridor. Mr Otis's youngest sons came out of their bedroom. The two young boys had the pillows from their beds in their hands. They threw the pillows at the ghost. They laughed at the ghost.

'Here is some Tammany Rising Sun Oil,' said Mr Otis.
'Please put the oil on your chains.'

The ghost was amazed and upset. No one had laughed at him before. He was a ghost. Everyone is frightened of ghosts. No one had ever laughed at the Canterville Ghost before.

The Canterville Ghost did not know what to do. He disappeared through the wall and the house became quiet.

The ghost went to the secret room where he lived. He sat down on a chair. He thought about what had happened.

He had frightened people for three hundred years. He had looked through windows and frightened the servants. He had knocked on bedroom doors. He had frightened people in their beds. He had blown out candles in the night. He had turned green and made noises with his chains. Everyone had always been frightened. No one had given him Rising Sun Oil to put on his chains. No one had thrown pillows at him. He was a very unhappy ghost.

---

Washington Otis removed the blood-stain in the library every day. Every morning the stain had reappeared. But the stain was no longer the colour of blood. One morning it was brown. Another morning it was purple. Then it became bright green.

The Otises laughed at the blood-stain. They looked for it every morning before breakfast.

'What colour is it today?' asked Washington Otis.

'It's green!' shouted the twins. 'It's green blood today.'

They laughed at the green blood-stain on the library floor.

Virginia Otis did not laugh. The young girl was silent at breakfast. The blood-stain made her feel sad and she almost cried when she saw the bright green stain. She was sure that the ghost put the stain on the floor. She felt sorry for the ghost.

'The stain has been here for three hundred years,' said Virginia. 'We have been here for three weeks. The poor ghost puts the stain on the floor every night. Can't you leave the stain there?'

But the others did not listen to Virginia.

———

The second appearance of the ghost was on a Sunday night. The Otises had all gone to bed. Suddenly they were woken up. They heard a terrible crashing noise downstairs.

The whole family ran out of their bedrooms. They ran downstairs. It was dark but Mr Otis and his eldest son carried candles. They heard another crashing noise in the hallway near the front door.

There was a suit of armour in the hallway. This suit of armour was more than three hundred years old. It had fallen over and made a loud noise. The Canterville Ghost was sitting on the floor next to the armour.

The ghost had tried to put on the suit of armour. He wanted to walk around the house and frighten the Otis family. But the metal suit was too heavy. The suit of armour had fallen onto the floor.

The Canterville Ghost was sitting beside the armour. He was rubbing his knee. He had hurt himself.

Mr Hiram B. Otis pointed a gun at the ghost. Washington Otis held his candle high in the air. The Otis twins laughed loudly. Virginia was afraid and stood beside her mother. They all looked at the Canterville Ghost.

*They all looked at the Canterville Ghost.*

The ghost was very angry. He stood up and gave a loud shout. He blew out the candle in Washington Otis's hand. There was no light in the hall. Then the ghost ran up the stairs in the darkness.

He stopped at the top of the stairs and laughed. He had a frightening laugh. Men's hair had turned grey when they heard him laugh. But the Otises were not afraid.

'Are you in pain?' asked Mrs Otis. 'I have a bottle of Dr Dobell's medicine. It is good for stomach-aches and headaches. Please take the medicine.'

The ghost looked at Mrs Otis angrily. Then he disappeared in a green cloud and went back to his secret room. He was very unhappy. He had tried to put on the suit of armour, but it was too heavy. The armour had fallen over and the ghost had hurt his leg.

The ghost stayed in his room during the day. He came out at night to visit the library. He repainted the blood-stain every night. And every morning, Washington Otis removed the blood-stain with Pinkerton's Stain Remover.

But the ghost had a problem. He had quickly finished all his red paint. Now his brown and purple paints were finished as well. So, sometimes he painted the blood-stain green, sometimes blue.

The ghost made plans. He wanted to frighten the Otis twins. He planned to visit the twins in the night. He planned to turn himself green and make a horrible noise. He planned to visit the twins in their bedroom. He planned to touch them with his ice-cold hands in the dark.

He left his secret room at midnight. The house was dark.

17

He climbed the stairs and walked along the corridor. The twins' bedroom was at the end of the corridor round a corner. He turned the corner. Suddenly he stopped.

In front of him was a round face with a terrible mouth and burning eyes. Fire shone out of the mouth and eyes of this horrible face. It was the face of a ghost!

The Canterville Ghost gave a shout and ran back to his secret room. He had never seen a ghost before and felt very frightened.

Before daylight came, the Canterville Ghost felt better. Were there two ghosts in the house? He must find out. He must meet the second ghost.

He went back upstairs and walked along the corridor towards the twins' room. The second ghost was still there, but its eyes were no longer burning. He went up to it. He touched it. The head of the second ghost fell onto the floor. It was not a ghost at all. It was a head made from a

large round vegetable called a pumpkin. The twins had put a candle inside it. There was a card on the floor.

> THE OTIS GHOST
> THE ONLY TRUE
> CANTERVILLE GHOST

The twins had put the head in the corridor to frighten him. This made the Canterville Ghost very angry. What could he do? He could think of nothing at that moment, so he went back to his room.

---

The ghost felt very weak and tired. He stayed in his room for five days. He did not repaint the blood-stain in the library. There had been a blood-stain on the library floor for three hundred years. Now the library floor was clean.

After a week the ghost felt better. He decided to try once more to frighten the Otis twins. He planned to make his face look as horrible as possible. He waited until the middle of the night.

Slowly and silently he walked to the twins' bedroom. It was one o'clock in the morning. The house was quiet. The door of the twins' room was slightly open.

The ghost took off his head and carried it under his arm. It is terrifying to see a headless ghost. He wanted to terrify the twins.

He pushed open the door of the twins' bedroom. The door banged against the wall.

He had planned to shout and hold his head in his hands. But a heavy jug of water fell from the top of the door. The twins had played a trick on him. He was soaked with water. The twins shouted and laughed.

The ghost ran back down the corridor. He could not frighten the twins. He could not frighten anyone in the Otis family.

Washington Otis came out of his bedroom. The ghost stopped running. Behind him, the twins ran down the corridor. They shouted – 'Boo!' – in his ears and waved their arms. Washington Otis laughed at him.

The ghost did not know what to do. He ran through the nearest door, went back to the secret room and lay down. He could not frighten anyone. He was a very unhappy ghost.

———

The Otises did not see the Canterville ghost at night again. The twins waited for him when it was dark. They put a rope across the corridor. They tied metal tins to the rope. But the ghost did not walk into the tins. Only Mr Otis came along the corridor. He fell over the rope and was very angry.

Virginia Otis was also angry with the twins. 'Can't you leave the poor ghost alone?' she said. 'Why do you want to hurt him? Why do you want to play tricks on him? He has lived here for a very long time. Leave him alone.'

The twins did not listen, but the ghost heard Virginia's words. The words gave him hope.

One afternoon, Virginia went to the library. The library door was slightly open. She pushed the door wide open and quietly walked into the room.

There was somebody sitting by the window. It was the Canterville Ghost!

He was looking at the library window which was made of

coloured glass. There were words painted on the glass.

He was wearing his best clothes and had combed his long grey hair.

'I feel very sorry for you,' said Virginia quietly. 'I'm sorry that my brothers were not very kind to you. But you did try to frighten them.'

'Yes I did,' said the ghost. 'It is my job to frighten everyone who comes to Canterville Chase.'

'You are very wicked, I know,' said Virginia, 'Mrs Umney, the housekeeper, told us that you killed your wife.'

'Yes I did,' replied the ghost. 'But she wasn't very kind. And it wasn't very kind of her brothers to starve me to death.'

'Starve you to death?' said Virginia. 'Oh, poor ghost, are you hungry? Would you like a sandwich?'

'No thank you,' he replied. 'I never eat anything. But you are very kind. You are much kinder than the rest of your family. They are rude, nasty and unkind.'

'Stop!' cried Virginia. 'You are nasty and unkind too. You stole my paint box. You used my paints to make the blood-stain in the library. I never told anyone about it. But now I'm going to fetch my father.'

She turned to go, but the ghost spoke again.

'Please do not go, Miss Virginia,' said the ghost. 'I am so lonely and so unhappy. I do not know what to do. I want to go to sleep and I cannot.'

'It's easy to sleep,' said Virginia. 'You go to bed and close your eyes.'

'I have not slept for three hundred years,' said the ghost. 'I have not slept since I was murdered by my wife's brothers.'

Virginia walked across the library and looked at the old face of the ghost. It was a sad face.

'Poor ghost,' said Virginia, 'how can I help you to sleep?'

'Far away in the woods,' said the ghost, 'there is a little garden. In the little garden the grass grows long and thick. There are many flowers and trees. A nightingale sings all night long. The bird's sweet song is beautiful and sad. The white stars and the pale moon look down on this little garden. It is very peaceful.'

Virginia's eyes were full of tears. She put her hands over her face.

'You mean it is the Garden of Death,' she said quietly.

'Yes, the Garden of Sleep,' said the ghost. 'It is very beautiful. There is peace and silence. There is no yesterday and no tomorrow. But only Love can open the door to the garden. For Love is stronger than Death.'

Virginia did not know what to say. She listened as the ghost spoke again.

'Have you read the writing on the library window?'

'Yes,' said Virginia, 'but I do not understand it.'

'Look,' said the ghost. 'Read the lines on the window.'

Virginia looked at the window and read the lines of poetry:

> When a golden girl shall weep
> For the ghost that cannot sleep,
> Then the dead at last shall die
> And in restful earth may lie.

'The words mean you must weep for me,' said the unhappy ghost. 'Then the Angel of Death will let me rest. Will you help?'

'What do I have to do?' asked Virginia.

'Look,' said the ghost. 'Read the lines on the window.'

'You must come with me into the darkness. You will see strange things. You will hear strange voices, but nothing will hurt you. You are good and kind. The dark cannot hurt you.'

Virginia did not answer and the ghost waited. He had waited for three hundred years. This was the longest minute of all that time.

'I am not afraid,' said Virginia at last. 'I will come with you into the dark.'

The ghost kissed her hand. His lips were cold like ice, but they burned like fire. The ghost held her hand and they walked to the wall of the library. The wall opened. There was darkness beyond the wall and a cold wind. Voices spoke out of the wind. 'Go back, Virginia. Go back before it is too late.'

Virginia walked into the darkness with the ghost. Virginia and the ghost disappeared through the library wall.

---

Virginia did not come downstairs for supper. Mr Otis sent one of the servants to her room. The servant could not find Virginia so everybody searched the house. They looked everywhere but they could not find her. Mr and Mrs Otis were very worried.

It was a summer evening and the sun had not set, so the family and the servants searched the gardens before it was dark. In the garden there were many trees and a deep pond. They looked in the pond. They looked in the trees. Then they asked people at the railway station. But no one had seen Virginia. Mr Otis went to tell the village policeman that Virginia had disappeared. But, by that time, it was dark and no one could search any more that night.

None of the family wanted to eat or sleep. They sat in the library and waited. They hoped Virginia would return safely. They planned to search for Virginia again in the morning.

It was midnight when the family decided to go to bed. They left the library and started to walk up the stairs together. Suddenly all the clocks in the house struck twelve and they heard a terrible noise. Thunder crashed outside the house and the Otises heard a dreadful cry. Strange music sounded inside the house and a door opened at the top of the stairs.

Virginia stood in the doorway. She looked down the stairs at them. Her face was very pale and she carried a small box in her hand.

'Where have you been?' Mr Otis asked angrily. 'Your mother has been very worried. You have frightened us all. You must never play a trick like this again.'

'Except on the ghost,' said the twins. 'You can play tricks on the ghost!'

'Father,' Virginia said quietly, 'I have been with the ghost. He is dead and now he can rest. He gave me this box of beautiful jewels before he died.'

She showed her father the small box. Inside was a necklace made of red stones.

'Where did you get this?' asked her father. 'Where have you been?'

Mr Otis forgot to be angry. He was so pleased to see that Virginia was safe.

'Come. I'll show you,' said Virginia.

She turned back to the door at the top of the stairs. All of the family followed her. Washington Otis carried a lighted candle.

Virginia led them along a secret corridor. They came to an old wooden door which was open. Beyond the door was a little room with a low ceiling. There was an iron ring in the wall and two chains. At the end of the chains was a body. Only bones remained. It was a skeleton.

'This is the body of Sir Simon de Canterville,' said Virginia. 'He murdered his wife in 1575. Then his wife's brothers shut him in this room. He was given no food. Sir Simon starved to death. His ghost was in this house for three hundred years. But now he has found peace.'

The Otis family looked around the little room and did not know what to say. Virginia knelt on the floor beside the skeleton and began to pray.

There was a funeral four nights later. The Otises buried the body of Sir Simon de Canterville in a grave among the trees.

*The Otises buried the body of Sir Simon de Canterville in a grave among the trees.*

The Otises, Mrs Umney the housekeeper, and all the servants from Canterville Chase stood near the grave. Behind them were people from the nearby village. Many people had come to the funeral.

Virginia carried white flowers. She looked up at the stars and the pale moon and the dark trees. She remembered what the ghost had said about the Garden of Death. A nightingale began to sing. The bird's sweet song was beautiful and sad.

Virginia smiled. 'God has forgiven him for murdering his wife,' she said.

# THE
# MODEL
# MILLIONAIRE

# THE MODEL MILLIONAIRE

Hughie Erskine was a good-looking man. Hughie Erskine was the best-looking gentleman in London. He had curly brown hair, grey eyes and a handsome face. He also had many friends.

However, Hughie Erskine did not have much money. His father had been an officer in the army. His father was dead. Now Hughie had his father's sword and a few books but no money.

Hughie Erskine had tried to do several jobs. He had worked for a tea merchant selling tea. He had worked for a wine merchant selling wine. But poor Hughie was not good at anything.

Hughie was in love and wanted to get married. He loved Laura Merton, the daughter of an army officer. Laura loved Hughie, but her father did not want them to get married.

'You are a fine young man,' Colonel Merton said to Hughie, 'but you have no money. My daughter cannot marry a man with no money. You may marry my daughter when you have ten thousand pounds.'

Hughie did not have ten thousand pounds. He did not have ten pounds. His old aunt gave him four or five pounds a week. Today he had only one pound in his pocket. Hughie was almost broke.

Hughie had a friend called Alan Trevor. Alan was an artist who painted pictures of people. He was a good artist and quite famous. Many people wanted him to paint their portrait. People came to Alan's studio. Alan painted their portraits in the studio. Alan's pictures were very expensive. He only painted pictures for rich men.

Hughie Erskine visited Alan Trevor in his studio. Alan was working on a painting.

'What do you think of this?' asked Alan Trevor. 'And what do you think of my model?'

Hughie looked at the painting. It was a picture of an old beggar. Alan was painting a picture of a man who was standing in the corner of the studio.

The model was an old man dressed in old, torn clothes. The old man's face was sad. With one hand he held out a hat. In the other hand he held a stick.

'My model is wonderful,' said Alan. 'Have you ever seen such a wonderful beggar?'

'Poor old man,' said Hughie. 'How sad he looks.'

'Of course,' said Alan. 'I don't want a beggar to look happy.'

'How much is a model paid for standing in your studio?' asked Hughie.

'Not much,' answered Alan, 'only a shilling an hour.'

'And how much money do you get when you sell a picture?' asked Hughie.

'For this picture, I will get two thousand pounds,' said Alan.

'You're a rich man. I think the model should get some of the money,' said Hughie.

'Nonsense … nonsense!' said Alan. 'It's difficult to be a painter. It's not difficult to be a beggar. Few people can paint pictures. Anyone can beg.'

'But many people want to be rich and famous painters,' said Hughie. 'No one wants to be a poor beggar. You artists are very unkind.'

'My model is wonderful,' said Alan. 'Have you ever seen such a wonderful beggar?'

Alan Trevor laughed. 'I'm busy,' he said. 'Sit down and stop talking.'

A servant came in. 'A gentleman is outside, sir. He wants you to paint his portrait. Can you speak to him, please?'

'Don't go away,' Alan said to Hughie. 'I'll be back in a moment.'

Alan left the room. The old beggar sat down on a chair and rested. His hat was still in his hand.

The old man looked so sad that Hughie felt sorry for him. Hughie put his hand in his pocket. He had a pound. It was the last of his money.

Well, he needs the money more than I do, thought Hughie.

Hughie went across the room and put the pound in the old man's hat.

The old man was very surprised. He looked at the money and smiled.

'Thank you, sir,' he said. 'Thank you very much.'

Alan Trevor came back into the studio and Hughie left. He went to see Laura and told her about the beggar.

'You gave all your money away?' said Laura. 'That was very foolish. My father will never let me marry a foolish man. You are very foolish, but you are very kind and I love you very much.'

That night Hughie met Alan Trevor at a club. Alan was looking very pleased.

'I finished that picture,' said Alan. 'And my model was very interested in you. He asked me lots of questions.'

'Poor old man,' said Hughie. 'I wish I could help him. What did he ask you about me?'

'He wanted to know everything about you,' said Alan.

'And what did you tell him?'

'I told him everything,' said Alan. 'I told him all about you. I told him about Laura. I told him about Laura's father. I told him you want to marry Laura but have no money.'

'Alan!' said Hughie angrily. 'You told him all about my private business?'

'Don't be angry,' said Alan. 'You don't know who I was painting the picture for. I was painting it for the Baron von Hausberg. He is one of the richest men in Europe. Baron von Hausberg was my model. The Baron dressed up as an old beggar.'

'The Baron von Hausberg!' cried Hughie. 'You mean that old beggar was the Baron himself?'

'Yes,' said Alan.

'But I gave him a pound,' said Hughie. 'Now I feel foolish.'

'You gave him a pound?' said Alan. 'That's the funniest thing I've ever heard.'

Alan Trevor could not stop laughing. Hughie Erskine walked home. He felt foolish. He had given his last pound to a millionaire. Laura's father would hear about this. The colonel would never let his daughter marry a fool.

The next day Hughie Erskine had a visitor. Hughie did not know the man.

'How can I help you?' asked Hughie.

'I have come from the Baron von Hausberg,' said the visitor.

'The Baron von Hausberg!' said Hughie Erskine. 'I did not know him when we met yesterday. I want to tell the Baron that I am sorry. I think I was rude to him.'

The visitor smiled. 'You were not rude to the Baron,' he said. 'The Baron asked me to give you this.' He gave Hughie an envelope.

Hughie thanked him and looked at the envelope. These words were written on the envelope: *A wedding present to Hugh Erskine and Laura Merton, from an old beggar.*

Inside was a cheque for ten thousand pounds.

# LORD
# ARTHUR SAVILE'S
# CRIME

# LORD ARTHUR SAVILE'S CRIME

'I want you to meet my palmist,' said Lady Windermere.

'What is a *palmist*?' asked Lord Arthur Savile.

'A palmist is a man who reads people's hands,' said Lady Windermere. 'A palmist can tell you your future by looking at your hand. It is important for a young man to know what his future will be.'

'Oh, you mean that he's an ordinary fortune-teller,' said Lord Arthur Savile.

'No, no,' said Lady Windermere quickly, 'he is not a *fortune-teller*. A palmist is much cleverer than a fortune-teller. Also palmists are more fashionable than fortune-tellers. Everyone in London wants to see a palmist. My palmist reads my hand every week.'

'Does he have a foreign name?' asked Lord Arthur.

'No, he is English,' Lady Windermere answered. 'His name is Mr Podgers.'

'Very well, please introduce me to Mr Podgers,' said Lord Arthur. 'But I do not want to know my future. I am happy with my life at the present time.'

They walked through a crowd of people. The room was full of ladies and gentlemen who were wearing fashionable and expensive clothes. They were all Lady Windermere's guests. This was Lady Windermere's Spring Reception. Lady Windermere's receptions were the most famous and fashionable parties in London. She had a reception every year and invited all the most famous and fashionable people in the capital.

There were several lords at the reception. Six government ministers were talking to a German Princess. The ministers smiled at Lady Windermere as she passed.

There were diplomats from many countries. There were famous artists and musicians and doctors. There was a fashionable scientist who talked about politics and economics. There was a Russian anarchist who talked about bombs. And there was Mr Podgers – the palmist.

'There he is,' said Lady Windermere. 'There is Mr Podgers. He is talking to the Duchess of Paisley.'

Lord Arthur Savile looked at Mr Podgers. Mr Podgers was looking at the Duchess of Paisley's hand. Mr Podgers was a short, fat man with an unpleasant smile. His eyes were small and bright and he wore gold spectacles. He held the Duchess's right hand and looked at it carefully.

'Your hand is beautiful, my lady,' he said. He smiled unpleasantly and bowed towards her.

Lord Arthur Savile looked at the Duchess's hand. It was small and ugly.

The Duchess waved her left hand and smiled at Mr Podgers.

'Your Ladyship is clever at business,' said Mr Podgers.

'When I married Lord Paisley I was a young woman,' said the Duchess. 'Lord Paisley had eleven castles and no houses. I made my husband sell the castles. Now I have twelve houses and no castles.'

Everyone laughed at this. Mr Podgers laughed most of all. Then everyone wanted Mr Podgers to look at their hands. But Lord Arthur Savile waited and watched.

Sir Thomas, the famous explorer, was next. He held out his hand and Mr Podger smiled.

'You have had many adventures,' said Mr Podgers. 'You

have been on four long sea voyages. Twice your ship has been sunk. You are planning another voyage – to the Antarctic. You had an illness when you were seventeen years old. You became rich when you were thirty. You do not like cats.'

'Amazing!' said Sir Thomas. 'Every word is true. It's quite amazing.'

'He reads the newspapers as well as hands,' Lady Windermere said to Lord Arthur. 'It is not difficult to tell the fortunes of famous people if you read the newspapers.'

'Then, you do not believe in fortune-telling,' said Lord Arthur. 'Why did you invite him to your reception?'

'I find him amusing,' Lady Windermere answered. 'He is fashionable and amuses the guests.'

Six, seven, eight people held out their hands to Mr Podgers. He read their hands and told them their future. Everyone was surprised and amazed.

They all laughed and talked loudly.

'Brilliant!'

'True!'

'Amazing!'

'Mr Podgers is wonderful.'

Mr Podgers read the hands of all the people around him. He smiled and promised good fortune. Only the Russian ambassador did not hold out his hand. Lord Arthur Savile waited and watched.

'Now, Lord Arthur, it is your turn,' said Lady Windermere. 'I want to know your future.'

'Why?' asked Lord Arthur.

'Because your fiancée Sybil is coming to see me tomorrow. You are getting married next month. I want to know that you will be happy. I will tell Sybil the good news.'

Lady Windermere spoke to Mr Podgers.

'Mr Podgers, here is Lord Arthur Savile. He is one of my favourite young men. He is getting married next month. Please tell him his future. Please tell him something good.'

Mr Podgers smiled at Lady Windermere. 'I will be pleased to do so, my lady.'

Mr Podgers held Lord Arthur's right hand. The palmist's face turned pale. He said nothing. He looked closely at Lord Arthur's hand for more than a minute.

Lord Arthur suddenly felt afraid. 'I am waiting, Mr Podgers,' he said.

'We are all waiting,' said Lady Windermere.

Mr Podgers took hold of Lord Arthur's left hand. He looked at it very closely. His gold spectacles almost touched Lord Arthur's hand. His face showed that he saw something horrible. But he looked up quickly and smiled unpleasantly.

'It is the hand of a very pleasant and charming young man,' said Mr Podgers.

'Of course it is,' said Lady Windermere angrily. 'But will he be a charming young husband? That's what I want to know.'

'All charming young men are charming husbands,' said Mr Podgers.

'I know that,' said Lady Windermere loudly. 'Tell me his future. What will happen in Lord Arthur's life?'

'There is little to tell,' said Mr Podgers. 'He will go on a journey … '

'Of course he will go on a journey,' said Lady Windermere. 'He is getting married next month. He and his wife will go on their honeymoon. Do you mean that? Do you mean his honeymoon?'

'I do not know ,' said Mr Podgers. 'Also, one of his relatives will die soon.'

'Who?' demanded Lady Windermere. 'Not his sister?'

'No, no, not a member of his close family. A distant relative,' said Mr Podgers. 'A distant cousin, perhaps.' Then he was silent. He said no more.

Lady Windermere was angry. This was a bad end to a wonderful evening.

'Come. It is time for supper,' Lady Windermere called to her guests. 'The food is ready.'

She walked out of the room. Everyone followed her to the supper table, except for Lord Arthur and Mr Podgers.

Lord Arthur looked at Mr Podgers angrily. Mr Podgers was afraid.

'Tell me what you saw in my hand,' said Lord Arthur. 'I am not a child. I must know the truth. Tell me now. I will pay you a hundred pounds.'

Mr Podgers' eyes shone brightly. A hundred pounds was a lot of money.

'Very well,' said Mr Podgers. 'Here is my address card.

MR SEPTIMUS R. PODGERS

*Professional Palmist*

103A WEST MOON STREET, LONDON

Please send a hundred pounds to my office tomorrow. Now I will tell you what I saw, but you will not like it.'

Lord Arthur Savile took the card. He listened while Mr Podgers told his fortune.

---

Ten minutes later, Lord Arthur Savile left Lady Windermere's house. He did not say goodbye to her. He was worried, upset – and afraid.

He walked away from the large house. He walked away from the fashionable street. All the houses in the street belonged to rich men.

He walked across Oxford Street and along the unfashionable streets in Soho. This was a poor part of London. A beggar asked for money as Lord Arthur passed. Two women with thick make-up on their faces laughed at him. He saw a fight in a dark street. He heard a scream from a dark, dirty building. Then a policeman stopped him.

'It's not safe for a gentleman to be walking along these streets at night,' said the policeman.

Lord Arthur thanked him and walked on. Lord Arthur saw another beggar. He put a coin in the old man's hand. This man was poor. Lord Arthur was rich. Was it this man's fortune to be poor? Was it Lord Arthur's fortune to be rich? Was a man's future written in his hand? Could Mr Podgers read that future?

Mr Podgers had read the future in Lord Arthur's hand. Could Lord Arthur escape his fate? No. Lord Arthur did not believe he could change the future. But perhaps he could make it happen in a different way?

Now Lord Arthur had walked to Marylebone. He did not know this part of London. He turned back towards Oxford Street. The streets were lit by gas lamps and fog came up from the river.

At the corner of Rich Street he saw two men. They were reading a police notice on the wall. Lord Arthur went up to

the notice and read it. He saw the word MURDER in large black letters. There had been a murder in Soho. The notice said the police would pay money for information. There was a drawing of the murderer on the notice.

Perhaps a police notice will show a drawing of me one day, thought Lord Arthur. It is my fate to be a murderer. Mr Podgers says that I will kill someone, soon.

---

Lord Arthur walked home to his house in Belgrave Square. He went to bed immediately and did not wake up until twelve o'clock the next day.

He thought about his fiancée, Sybil. Her photograph was beside his bed. They were going to be married in a month and he loved her.

He also thought about what Mr Podgers had told him. 'You will kill someone,' Mr Podgers had said.

'But who will I kill?' Lord Arthur had asked. Mr Podgers had said nothing.

Why did he believe the palmist? It was strange. He had felt afraid when Mr Podgers spoke. Lord Arthur believed that the palmist's words were true. 'I will kill someone,' he said. It was simple. But who? Where? When? The questions went round and round in his head.

Lord Arthur Savile decided two things. The first was that he could not marry Sybil – not yet. The second was this – 'I will make my own future. I will kill someone,' he said. Perhaps the decisions were strange, but Lord Arthur had decided what to do.

Mr Podgers had said something else. 'One of your relatives will die soon … a distant relative, perhaps a distant cousin.' Lord Arthur did not have many distant relatives. There was only his second cousin, Lady Clementina Beauchamp. She was an old lady who lived in Curzon Street. Lord Arthur decided to kill her. 'She is old and will not live long,' he said. 'I will kill her. Then I will marry Sybil.'

He went to a large library and looked at the books on medicine. A book called *Toxicology* helped him. It was a book about poisons. There was a strong poison called *aconitine* which worked quickly and painlessly. Lord Arthur wrote down the name of the poison then went to a pharmacy.

Lord Arthur asked to see the pharmacist. 'I have a large dog,' Lord Arthur said the pharmacist. 'It has bitten several people. I must kill the dog, but I do not want to shoot it. Can you help me? I need a quick and painless poison. My doctor told me there is a poison called aconitine.'

'Yes, there is a poison called aconitine,' said the pharmacist, 'but I cannot give it to you. You must bring a signed paper from your doctor. I need a certificate from a doctor before I can give you the poison.'

'My doctor is Sir Matthew Reid and I am Lord Arthur Savile. Do I have to get a certificate? I am leaving the country very soon and I am in a hurry.'

The pharmacist had heard the name, Sir Matthew Reid. Sir Matthew Reid was a famous doctor. 'Well, my lord, if you promise you will only use the poison to kill this dog …'

'Yes, of course,' said Lord Arthur, 'I promise.'

'Very well,' said the pharmacist. 'I will make a pill of poison for your dog.'

The pharmacist made the poison pill. It looked like a small, round sweet. Half an hour later, Lord Arthur bought a small box of sweets in a shop in Piccadilly. He threw the sweets away and put the poison pill in the box. Then he went to visit Lady Clementina Beauchamp.

'Arthur! I'm so happy to see you,' said Lady Clementina. 'How is Sybil? Is everything ready for your marriage?'

'Sybil is very well, thank you,' said Lord Arthur. 'She has gone to see Lady Windermere today. I am going to see Sybil later.'

'You are very kind to visit me,' said Lady Clementina. 'I am old and ill. I'm sure you young people think I am boring. My only visitor is the doctor.'

'I know you are not well,' said Lord Arthur. 'I have brought you some medicine.'

He gave the sweet box to Lady Clementina who looked inside. She took out the pill and looked at it.

'It looks like a sweet,' Lady Clementina said. 'Are you sure it is medicine? Shall I take it now?'

'It is medicine … yes … but do not take it now,' said Lord Arthur. 'It is a new medicine from America. It is a very good medicine. Take it before you go to bed. It will help you to sleep.'

'You are very kind,' said Lady Clementina. 'I will try to remember to take it. I am old and I forget many things. But I will not forget to come to your wedding.'

Lord Arthur said goodbye to Lady Clementina. Then he went to see Sybil at her father's house in Park Lane. He wanted to change the date of their marriage. He wanted to delay their marriage, but he did not want to hurt Sybil.

Lord Arthur asked Sybil to wait. 'We will be married …

but not yet. Please wait a little longer. Everything will be all right. Believe me.'

Sybil was very unhappy. She did not understand. Why did Arthur want to delay their marriage? Lord Arthur sat and talked with her until late in the evening. Then he took the midnight train to Venice in Italy.

———

In Venice, Lord Arthur met his brother, Lord Surbiton. They were together for two weeks but Lord Arthur did not enjoy his visit to Venice. He was worried and restless. He read the newspapers from England every day. He looked for news of Lady Clementina Beauchamp.

One morning a message arrived from London. Lady Clementina was dead. She had said she wanted Lord Arthur to have her house. So Lord Arthur Savile now owned Lady Clementina's house.

Lord Arthur returned to London at once. First he went to see Sybil and make plans for their wedding. Then he and Sybil went to Lady Clementina's house.

Lord Arthur and Sybil looked around Lady Clementina's house. They opened drawers and cupboards. In one drawer Sybil found a small sweet box.

'Look at this lovely little box,' Sybil said to Arthur. 'It has an old sweet inside it.'

Lord Arthur looked. His face turned pale. It was the box he had given to Lady Clementina. The poison pill was still inside.

'I will throw it away,' said Lord Arthur. He took the pill and threw it on the fire.

'But don't burn the box,' said Sybil. 'Please don't throw

'Look at this lovely little box,' Sybil said to Arthur. 'It has an old sweet inside it.'

the box away. Arthur, you look very pale. Is anything wrong?'

Lord Arthur knew he had not killed Lady Clementina. He had decided to kill someone before his marriage. Now he had to delay his marriage again.

---

Lord Arthur Savile delayed his marriage for the second time. Sybil was very upset. Her father was angry. Lord Arthur Savile was very unhappy.

Lord Arthur had to find someone to murder. He had no more distant relatives. So he decided to murder a close member of his family, his uncle, the Dean of Chichester. His uncle was an important man in the Church.

The Dean was interested in clocks. He had a large collection of clocks. So, Lord Arthur decided to send him a bomb inside a clock. But where could he find a bomb?

He remembered Lady Windermere's reception. He had met a young Russian called Count Rouvaloff. The Count had talked about anarchism and bombs. There was often news of anarchists in the newspapers. Anarchists killed important people with bombs. Lord Arthur knew that the Count lived near the British Museum. He went to visit him.

'You want a bomb?' said the Count. 'I did not know you were interested in politics.'

'I have some private business. I'm not interested in politics,' said Lord Arthur.

Count Rouvaloff looked at him in surprise. He thought that only anarchists used bombs. But he saw Lord Arthur was serious. He believed that Lord Arthur did want a bomb. He wrote an address on a piece of paper.

'This is a secret address,' said Count Rouvaloff. 'Tell no one. Read this address then burn the paper.'

'I shall burn it, do not worry,' said Lord Arthur.

He shook the Russian's hand then left. The paper gave an address in Soho. Soho was a poor part of London where many foreign people lived. Lord Arthur went to Greek Street. He knocked on the door of an old building.

The man who opened the door spoke German. Lord Arthur showed him the paper from Count Rouvaloff.

'Come in,' said the man.

The building was an empty shop. Lord Arthur waited for a few minutes. Then another man came into the room.

'My name is Herr Winckelkopf,' said the man. 'How can I help you?'

'My name is Smith,' said Lord Arthur. 'Count Rouvaloff sent me. I need a bomb.'

'What kind of a bomb?' asked Herr Winckelkopf.

'A bomb in a clock,' said Lord Arthur.

'Ah, I sent a bomb in a clock to the governor of Odessa,' said Herr Winckelkopf. 'Who do you want to blow up?'

'I want to blow up the Dean of Chichester.'

'A churchman? So, you are interested in religion.'

'No, it is private business.'

'I have a beautiful clock,' said Herr Winckelkopf. He showed a clock to Lord Arthur. There were two wooden figures on the clock – a woman and a dragon. 'The woman is Liberty,' continued Herr Winckelkopf. 'The dragon is Dictatorship. Liberty is stronger than Dictatorship.'

'Yes, I understand,' said Lord Arthur. 'But I am not interested in politics. Can you make the bomb immediately?'

'I have an important job to do for friends in Moscow,' said Herr Winckelkopf. 'But I can make your bomb in a few days. When do you want it to explode?'

'On Friday, at midday.'

Lord Arthur wrote an address on a piece of paper. 'Please send it to the Dean of Chichester. Here is the address.'

'Friday, at midday,' repeated Herr Winckelkopf. 'The Dean of Chichester.'

'And how much money do I owe you?' asked Lord Arthur.

'I do not work for money,' said Herr Winckelkopf. 'I'm an anarchist. I'm working for Liberty. Please pay me five pounds.'

Lord Arthur paid him five pounds and left the house in Greek Street. He waited at home until the weekend. He waited for news.

The weekend came. Nothing happened. He waited

another week. Still nothing happened. Then he received a letter from the Dean of Chichester.

> *The Deanery,*
> *Chichester*
>
> *Dear Arthur,*
> *I am writing to ask you about London fashions. Last week I received a clock, but I do not know who sent it. It is a clever toy. It has an alarm inside like a small hammer. When the alarm strikes twelve, smoke comes out of the clock. It is very clever. Does everyone in London have a clock like this?*
>
> *Your Uncle*

Lord Arthur had not killed his uncle. The bomb had not worked. He was very worried. 'What shall I do?' he asked himself. 'Shall I leave the country? Shall I tell Sybil I will not marry her?'

That evening he went out to dinner with his brother, Lord Surbiton. His brother's friends were young and foolish. They made a lot of noise in the restaurant. Lord Arthur became bored with their conversation. He left the restaurant at eleven o'clock and walked beside the river.

A fog was coming off the river. The street lamps along the road shone like silver moons. There were few people on the streets. Lord Arthur walked from Blackfriars towards Westminster. He heard Big Ben – the huge clock at Westminster – strike twelve o'clock. Lord Arthur stood by the wall and looked down at the river. The fog was thick and he could not see the river easily. The light of the street lamps made the river black and silver. The water was moving quickly. The river made Lord Arthur think of dark and terrible things.

He hated Mr Podgers the palmist. He had been happy before he knew his fate. 'I know I will kill someone,' Lord Arthur said to himself. 'It is my fate. Why did Mr Podgers tell me? I was happy. I did not want to know my future.'

He looked away from the river and saw something moving in front of him. He walked on. There was something strange in front of him. A man was leaning over the wall. Was he going to jump into the river?

Lord Arthur walked forward quickly. Then he stopped.

A street lamp was shining on the man's face. It was Mr Podgers the palmist! Lord Arthur had a clever idea.

Lord Arthur ran forward quickly and quietly. He took hold of Mr Podgers by the legs and pushed him over the wall. There was a cry and a splash, then silence.

Lord Arthur stood by the wall and looked down. He could not see Mr Podgers.

'Have you dropped something, sir?' asked a voice behind him suddenly.

He turned round and saw a policeman with a lamp.

'It was nothing important, sergeant,' Lord Arthur answered, smiling.

Lord Arthur suddenly felt very happy. Now he had no more worries.

---

*He took hold of Mr Podgers by the legs and pushed him over the wall.*

A day later Lord Arthur read a report in The Times newspaper.

# SUICIDE OF A PALMIST

The body of Mr Septimus R. Podgers was found in the River Thames yesterday. Mr Podgers was a famous palmist.

Police questioned Mr Podgers' friends. They said that Mr Podgers had been working very hard. Mr Podgers was writing a book about reading palms. His friends thought he had become ill because he worked so hard.

The police believe that Me Podgers killed himself by jumping into the River Thames.

Lord Arthur ran out of the house and went to Sybil's house in Park Lane. Sybil was looking out of the window. When she saw Arthur in the street, she ran downstairs to meet him.

'Sybil, let us get married tomorrow,' Arthur shouted. 'No … not tomorrow … Let's get married today!'

'You foolish boy!' Sybil was laughing and crying at the same time. She and Arthur were both very happy.

———

After their wedding, Arthur and Sybil visited Lady Windermere.

'Are you happy?' asked Lady Windermere.

'We are both very happy,' said Arthur. 'And we hope that you are too.'

'I have no time to be happy,' said Lady Windermere. 'I am always looking for new people to invite to my receptions.'

'I read in the newspaper that Mr Podgers, your palmist, is

dead,' said Arthur.

'Oh, Mr Podgers …' replied Lady Windermere. 'There is a new fashion now. It is called *telepathy*. I have a telepathist who reads peoples' minds. I became tired of Mr Podgers. He could not read the future. He never told me anything useful. I did not believe him.'

'I believed him,' said Arthur. 'Everything he told me was true. He has made me very happy!'

'How has he made you happy?' asked Lady Windermere in surprise.

Arthur looked into his wife's eyes and said, 'He has helped me to marry Sybil.'

'What nonsense!' cried Lady Windermere. 'I never heard such nonsense.'

# Points for Understanding

## THE CANTERVILLE GHOST

1  Who is Mr Hiram B. Otis?
2  Why does Mr Hiram B. Otis meet Lord Canterville?
3  'I don't believe in ghosts,' says Mr Otis.
   Why does he say this?
4  Mr Hiram B. Otis and Lord Canterville make an agreement.
   What is this agreement?
5  What do you know about Mr Hiram B. Otis's children?
6  Who is Mrs Umney?
7  Describe the library at Canterville Chase.
8  'What is this red stain?' Mrs Otis asks Mrs Umney. What does
   Mrs Umney tell her about the stain?
9  'I have some Pinkerton's Stain Remover,' says Washington
   Otis.
   (a)  What does he do?
   (b)  What does Mrs Umney do?
   (c)  What does Mrs Umney tell the Otises?
10 Why does Mr Otis want to find the ghost?
11 Mr Otis gets out of bed and opens the bedroom door.
   (a)  Why does Mr Otis wake up?
   (b)  What does he see when he opens the door?
   (c)  What does Mr Otis do?
12 The ghost is amazed and upset. Why?
13 The ghost has frightened people for three hundred years.
   How has he frightened them?
14 Washington Otis removes the blood-stain every day.
   (a)  What happens to the blood-stain?
   (b)  What do the twins do when they see the blood-
        stain ?
   (c)  How does Virginia feel?
15 The ghost appears for the second time on a Sunday night.
   (a)  Where does he appear?
   (b)  How do the Otises know that the ghost is there?
   (c)  What does the ghost do when he sees the Otises?
   (d)  How does the ghost feel?

16  The twins play two tricks on the ghost. What are the two tricks?
17  Where is the ghost when Virginia meets him?
18  What does the ghost tell Virginia about himself?
19  Why does Virginia get angry with the ghost?
20  Where does the ghost want to go?
21  The ghost tells Virginia to read the words on the library window.
    (a)  What do the words mean?
    (b)  What must Virginia do to help the ghost?
    (c)  Where do Virginia and the ghost go together?
22  Virginia does not come downstairs for supper.
    (a)  Where do the Otises and the servants look for Virginia?
    (b)  Who do they ask about Virginia?
23  What happens at midnight?
24  Where does Virginia take her family? What does she show them?
25  Describe the funeral of Sir Simon de Canterville.


## THE MODEL MILLIONAIRE

1  What do you learn about Hughie Erskine in the first four paragraphs of this story?
2  Why doesn't Colonel Merton want Hughie to marry Laura?
3  When will the Colonel let Hughie marry Laura?
4  Alan Trevor is an artist.
    (a)  What kind of pictures does he paint?
    (b)  Who does he paint pictures for?
5  Hughie goes to visit Alan Trevor. Alan is painting a picture. Who is he painting a picture of?
6  'You artists are very unkind.'
   Why does Hughie say this to Alan?
7  Why does Hughie give the old beggar all his money?
8  Hughie and Alan meet at a club. Why does Hughie become angry with Alan?
9  Alan tells Hughie that the old beggar is the Baron von Hausberg.
    (a)  How does Hughie feel?
    (b)  Why does Alan laugh at Hughie?

10 The next day a man comes to visit Hughie.
    (a)    Who has sent the man to visit Hughie?
    (b)    Why has the man come?
11 Why has the Baron von Hausberg sent a cheque to Hughie?


## LORD ARTHUR SAVILE'S CRIME

1 Who is Mr Podgers? What is his job?
2 What does Mr Podgers do at Lady Windermere's Spring Reception?
3 How does Lord Arthur know that Lady Windermere does not believe in fortune-telling?
4 Why has Lady Windermere invited Mr Podgers to her reception?
5 Why does Lady Windermere want Mr Podgers to read Lord Arthur's hand?
6 The palmist looks at Lord Arthur's hand and his face turns pale. Why?
7 Why does Lady Windermere become angry with Mr Podgers?
8 Why does Mr Podgers agree to tell Lord Arthur's fortune?
9 Lord Arthur sees a police notice on a wall.
    (a)    What does the notice show?
    (b)    What does the notice make Lord Arthur think about?
10 Lord Arthur thinks about what Mr Podgers told him. Then he makes two decisions. What are these two decisions?
11 Who does Lord Arthur decide to kill and why?
12 What does Lord Arthur find out at the library?
13 Why does the pharmacist agree to give Lord Arthur some poison?
14 What does Lord Arthur do with the poison?
15 Why does Lord Arthur go to visit Sybil?
16 Lord Arthur goes to Venice. Why does he read the newspapers from England every day?
17 Sybil finds a small sweet box in a drawer at Lady Clementina's house. What does Arthur do with the box?
18 'Arthur, you look very pale,' says Sybil.
Why is Lord Arthur pale?
19 Who does Lord Arthur decide to murder now?

20 Who is Count Rouvaloff? Why does Lord Arthur visit him?
21 What is Herr Winckelkopf going to do for Lord Arthur?
22 Lord Arthur receives a letter from the Dean of Chichester.
    (a) What does the Dean tell him?
    (b) Has Lord Arthur's plan succeeded?
23 Why does Lord Arthur go for a walk by the river?
24 As he walks by the river, Lord Arthur thinks about Mr Podgers. Why does he hate Mr Podgers?
25 Who does Lord Arthur see leaning over the wall?
26 What does Lord Arthur do? How does he feel?
27 Lord Arthur reads a newspaper report.
    (a) What does he learn about Mr Podgers?
    (b) What does he do next?
28 Why doesn't Lady Windermere care about Mr Podgers any more?
29 'He has helped me to marry Sybil,' says Lord Arthur. What does Lord Arthur mean by these words?

Road to Nowhere *by John Milne*
The Black Cat *by John Milne*
Don't Tell Me What To Do *by Michael Hardcastle*
The Runaways *by Victor Canning*
The Goalkeeper's Revenge and Other Stories *by Bill Naughton*
The Stranger *by Norman Whitney*
The Promise *by R. L. Scott-Buccleuch*
The Man With No Name *by Evelyn Davies and Peter Town*
The Cleverest Person in the World *by Norman Whitney*
Claws *by John Landon*
Z for Zachariah *by Robert C. O'Brien*
Tales of Horror *by Bram Stoker*
Frankenstein *by Mary Shelley*
Silver Blaze and Other Stories *by Sir Arthur Conan Doyle*
Tales of Ten Worlds *by Arthur C. Clarke*
The Boy Who Was Afraid *by Armstrong Sperry*
Room 13 and Other Ghost Stories *by M. R. James*
The Narrow Path *by Francis Selormey*
The Woman in Black *by Susan Hill*

For further information on the full selection of
Readers at all five levels in the series, please refer
to the Macmillan Readers catalogue.

Published by Macmillan Heinemann ELT
Between Towns Road, Oxford OX4 3PP
Macmillan Heinemann ELT is an imprint of
Macmillan Publishers Limited
Companies and representatives throughout the world

ISBN 0 435 27212 8

First published 1993
This retold version by Stephen Colbourn for Macmillan Guided Readers
Design and illustration © Macmillan Publishers Limited 2002
Heinemann is a registered trademark of Reed Educational and Professional Publishing Limited
This version first published 2002

Illustrated by Annabel Large
Cover by Bee Willey and Threefold Design

Printed in China

2006 2005 2004 2003 2002
20 19 18 17 16 15 14 13